Behind
the
Mask

w.g. murray

authorHOUSE®

AuthorHouse™
1663 Liberty Drive
Bloomington, IN 47403
www.authorhouse.com
Phone: 833-262-8899

Published by AuthorHouse 12/16/2020

ISBN: 978-1-6655-0920-6 (sc)
ISBN: 978-1-6655-0919-0 (e)

Print information available on the last page.

This book is printed on acid-free paper.

This book was written for

my children

Allison, Leah and Ronan

So you will know

Love brought you here
and
Love will take you home.

Remember Love….

Contents

Madness 1

Bread and Circuses 2

Disorder 3

A Jail of Choice 4

The Light of the World 5

Behind the Mask 6

The Mind's Return 7

Life's Meaning 8

The Only Certainty 9

Insanity 10

Confusion 11

Random Thoughts 12

Dysfunction 14

Insufficient 16

Irrational 17

Error 18

Suffering 19

Sabotage 20

Montreal on time… 21

The Mask of Self 22

The Pandemia 23

What ensued? 24

The Resistant Heart 25

Little One 26

Who am I? 27

Fear 28

Thought Police 29

Nothing Matters 30

The Incarceration of Belief 31

Alive 32

Helpless 33

The Imprisoned Forgotten 34

Fear..35

Change of Mind...36

The Fight...37

The Night..38

The Cross..39

The Notebooks 40

The Circle Game..41

Freedom..43

Death of Illusion 44

Acceptance 45

Perfection 46

Redemption 47

The Christ Before Me 48

You...49

The Unseen..51

Pyramid 53

All there is...54

Kindness 56

Turn from it 57

The Christ in Me 58

Salvation 59

Of My Life...60

The Word After 61

Meditation 62

Madness

It moved in like madness
From the East.
Only God knows why.

The telescreen said
"Be scared
Stay inside
Where death and disease
Will not find you."

The words are said
So, they must be true

Within the guilt, conspiracy, and blame
The world stopped
And, like sheep, we followed each other
Into the pit of madness.

Chaos
Confinement
Release
Freedom
Creation

It's all here.
Remove the mask.
Find Yourself.

Bread and Circuses

The truth is never spoken
The great men have all declined
Sucked in by 'bread and circuses'
And the safety of the silent mind

It's the sycophant of illusion
A refusal to see what is real.
Chained to the ego, in madness
within this place all I think is fear

Voices echo – back and forth
The words unclear, unmeant
As the shadows dance
The illusion is what is made
And I defend against it as real

The only escape is Surrender
To the truth beyond all fiction
Turn to kindness, turn to love
Focus on heaven
On the inside.

Disorder

It was getting dark outside
My light was fading in the coldness
It's all scum and nuts
If it's going well … you know
it will all be over soon.

here
too scared to go out
into the threat
It's a blessing or a curse
everything or nothing …

From the impossible stench
day after day
With as much defeat as you can get
Even the rocks have had enough.

Days and days of silent screaming
With the door locked
Pillow over your head
And the dresser up against the door.

Don't go out!! Don't go out!!
There's nothing out there
Not even forgiveness.

A Jail of Choice

Life's fundamental shift.
The planet changed.
Life stopped.
Everyone wore the masks of the Pandemic
in fear of spreading a flu called COVID-19.
Contagion, fear, blame, shame...
the hallmarks of the human race.
   Imagine...
These walls are made of steel,
and I can't get out.
All I hear is the sound of the lock "click"
and my hand grips the solid bar
of the cage as I shake it.
The jailer with the key looks at me,
shakes her head and walks away.
There is no way out.
So, I turn to the little telescreen
on the wall next to my bed and turn it on.
This is distraction.
This is delusion.
Through it all things are made.

We are all in a jail of our own choosing.
We walk the path of least resistance.
Tear off the mask; your face is beautiful.

The Community of God is gone.
Replaced with fear.

You are the Creator of your Life

The Light of the World

The light of Love
Shines down on God's creation
And in compassion, smiles with courage
At the hopeless thoughts of you
In a world that seems forgotten.

Your faith and trust are sanctified
As the spirit guides your every step
Seek his guidance in the silence
Far away from the chaos of this world.

Learn to trust the guidance of He
Who knows your soul and spirit's song
Love each other – help those around you
Work together – for me and through me
In peace and harmony – for one is the same

Begin each day in peace and silence
Go forth in love in truth, sharing peace
Bring all of the earth joy in my name
The Christ and your true self
One and the same

Behind the Mask

Hidden
Behind the mask
your spirit
the reality of you
waits
In the stillness of everyday

You already are
What you need to be
In this life
There is nothing
That could ever affect
Your true being

The Father has willed
Your creation
You are as He has made.
Immortal
Untouchable
Fully loved.
Only God's creation is real
Trust him.
And that is
all
That is.

The Mind's Return

The Nor 'wester blew cold
Through the old windows that wouldn't close
Of the green, shingled farmhouse
On the bank of the sea.

Through cups of tea and suffering
Blame, guilt and fear
Work to be worthy
Of myself, I am not enough.

Crowded in – left for nothing
No attention, anger learned at an early age
I crawled out of that mess
And now I'm free.

Question the thoughts that seem to cause you pain
Is that true? Or for my ego's gain?
Don't force yourself to be loved or liked.
Your truth will appear if you let the love in.

On the side of those who struggle, all are good
you know it's true.
Speak the truth of yourself always,
Let the Holy Spirit work through you.

Life's Meaning

You are not useless. You are not a disease on the planet
Pick up your life and carry it.
Take care of yourself and those who rely on you.
Be responsible; Make your life mean something.
Rise to your life, rise to its challenge!
Refuse to live in shame.
Don't swim at the bottom. Rise to the top and be an example.
This life is not your right or your freedom, it's your opportunity!
This life is your creation! Be optimistic!! Be strong!!
And the truth is, your life is your responsibility – no one else's
That is the secret to meaning. That you rose above yourself.
That you created something good. That you are a success!
That you were there when people needed you…
Within the darkness that seems all around,
Reveal the best of yourself.
On any given day anything can happen,
And you must rise prepared for that.
You are not useless, you are not evil, you are courageous
<u>YOU</u> ARE an indomitable force for good in this world.
Set your ambition higher; inspire creativity and courage in those around you
Help others bear witness to greater meaning in their lives.
Challenge yourself to be limitless…decide who you want to be
Decide upon the life you want to have…
Take on the challenge, God only knows what you can achieve if you try
….*so, try*

The Only Certainty

You are not alone
You are not without hope
God's love for you is constant and certain
Trust in God
He will not leave you
You are created through the thought of God
That creation has never abandoned you
It is here; with you and me.
It is eternal as are you.
This is the rule of life.
You are one with creation
You could never leave it
The thought of God protects you,
And lights your path.

You have everything you need
For what purpose do we deny ourselves
Happiness, joy, healing and peace?
Many search the broad horizon
And beseech God for help
All is given to you – in your hands
Yet you say you do not have it.
When acceptance is given by you
And you lie sated after the journey to salvation
You will see the power of the Christ consciousness
To heal the mind to recognize the spirit that God created.

Insanity

We are stuck here
In our own misery
Pretending this is real
And the doctors
And the lawyers
Make their money
And go to their fancy homes
And put their well-polished shoes
Up on their expensive footstools
And drink imported Scotch
From Irish crystal.

And the pints flow
And the drunkards go
In and out of the public houses
Hoping for something better
Pretending to care

And the dating sites fill
And the retirement homes fill
And the shopping malls fill
And the asylums fill
And the cemeteries fill

It seems that Nothing stays
The illusion is that Everything goes
Could it be that all is madness?

Confusion

I smell the desperation
The lonely man
And the lonely woman
Eating alone
Drinking alone
Loving alone

There is such loneliness in this world
You see it in the eyes
Of people sitting on park benches
In the empty churches
The empty dinner tables

Searching for some time
Some thing
Some way
That it will all make sense…

But it doesn't
Because you created
Your life
This way.

Random Thoughts

Uncertainty and fear
Enter your mind

But the One
Of creation
Cannot be stifled
by the marks of ego.

The road
Seems long
The loneliness of life
Mocks and saddens

But of Holiness
Life is expression
Of who we are
As love.

But of Stillness
To come to
The ultimate
Realization
Of who we are.

But of Peace
The sorrow ends
And the construct
Is unmade
All uncertainty will turn to dust

When you are ready
illusions of this life will fade
and you will know all that is
Love
In the embrace of our Father.

Dysfunction

The innocence of the child
Slapped repeatedly – pulled here and there
Until it believes
It is unlovable, unwanted.
Through tear soaked, dirty face and messy hair:
The little body is taught to crave the love
that this world falsely teaches is outside itself.
Self-hatred, guilt and shame
rise in the little body
With the spirit hidden inside that is
Of such magnitude, beloved by God

Searching the world for a reason not to be loved
you act out your play of self-hatred
when in truth: all love lies within
The value and identity of God, our Father,
could never be challenged by the thoughts of others
Neither can yours.
God, in tears, admonishes us
Do not believe that you are what I am not
I am love and therefore so are you.

You are as God created you
And you can never be less than that.
There is enough love in you
To turn the sky blue and fill the earth with life.
Turn your love inward
and let go of the thought of emptiness
Recognize when you close your eyes
the love that is God, and truth

There is nothing else
God's love is you. One and the same.

You are perfect as God created you.
You need nothing
But to accept that truth.
The beliefs of others are unimportant.
Remember who you are.
You are sacred and loved beyond measure.

Insufficient

There is nothing wrong with me
As the search for purpose draws to an end.
And play important games
In this, the ego's playground.

As the young women seek
success and belonging
and the protection
of the immeasurable heaven

Given away, to walk down the aisle.
In their fancy, gowns in a virgin white
And textbook hair
Made up for the day of perfection.
It's a rite of passage;
A balm to the superficial ego.
The hallmark of success
Achievement
Somebody special loves me.
Therefore, I am of value.

This is not success;
This is what you think you want.
Following after delusion
To make a show of self
To impress people, even those you don't like…

Irrational

The telescreen says
Be scared of life
And go and come in fear
How can you hear
The voice for God
When the news media ignorance
Is blasting through your ears
The world you see
Reflected to you remains believed.
Corporations pay to ramp up the emotion
Then show you a commercial
In psychological manipulation.
The interchangeable contestants
Match up for the show
And we do not fully question
What is shown to you;
Through the eyes of the body

Who will make a difference?
Your flimsy faith is placed
In what your senses report.
Your hands do not touch the reality of truth.
To you, it seems more real than God.
In the silence of this one
Moment of stillness.
Let the voice of God create your reality.
Give Him your thoughts
And watch as they are transformed
In sanctity; To miracles.

Error

In the obvious awareness of the day
The little girl stood plain as could be
In the middle of the yard behind the big barn.

Without the ability to understand
Where she was, and why…
She looked up to the sky for God.
"Where are you, Papa?"
She still remembered love

In the sky, that is where she is told God is.
The God of the Bible
The only one she thinks she knows.
She tried to reason it through
For reason sees through errors
Telling her that she was mistaken in
what she thought was real

Looking down at the ground,
It seems solid enough
Mamma said she's full of sin
And there is no way out.
She goes to church
Yet she cannot pray
For no one taught her how
And how can anyone be listening
To a little girl with dirty feet
Who doesn't matter.

Suffering

The martyr
Consumed
With the addiction to suffering
It's all she has
When she believes that she
Is a victim of the world;
This world is all there is and
Madness has no end.

The martyr
Makes herself so busy
That she can't hear the Voice of God

She attacks, she hurts, she's not understood
Unfairly treated, constantly in lack
There seems no way out
She sees her essence as weak, vulnerable and separate
She cannot rest in the only thing that would heal it:
Forgiveness.

She will not turn to the Father for love
She will not admit defeat.
And she will not ask the Holy Spirit's direction.
In stubborn complacency, she assigns guilt to all

Forgiveness ends all suffering
Turn to God and let Him remove it.
Father I return my mind to you.

Sabotage

How do I claim freedom?
When all around me are judgement and guilt.
Born into this place. Alone. Helpless. Misunderstood.
What is success?
I am admired by people I don't like,
And I have so many things I don't want.
I drink too much because I have to,
To help me sleep until morning comes.
This can't be real. I act the part..
It's all a mask I hide behind
No one wants to see the reality of me.

I dress the part of what is wanted.
A response to unreality.
Long years after the dream began.
I came to God on bended knee.
I asked for help and he answered wholly.
Calm, serene, peaceful.

Reality is on the inside.

It matters that we are here.

Montreal on time...

The air felt heavy
Like a tarp
Or a weighted blanket
an unwanted love affair
Too easy to embrace
But
The glue of lack
Sticks heavy

The ease was absent
In the cinderblock hotel
That stood as an excuse for luxury
In the middle of a concrete barren.

At the restaurant
They served breakfast for free
To compensate for the noise
Of the black brotherhood
Undisciplined in screams
Waking us from sleep at 3 am

And I lay back
Onto my lumpy pillow
Listening to the world change
Into something
I had never seen before.

Find your Purpose and Do it!

The Mask of Self

The illusion of me
Covers my heart
And
Won't let me speak
'O soul'
Lives imprisoned within

The darkness abiding
Mythological sin

Where is truth?
Lost within

Among the hatred
Ego and lies

In deceit and mockery
Down the smoky old hall
Of distraction and delusion

The mask covers all.

The Pandemia

What does it mean?
Impermanence
The reality of guilt
Projected to you
And at you

It's been a long night
But nature grew
In silence
The long minutes
The hours
In the curfew of life

While the many stayed inside.
Alone
The earth stopped and rested
To a greater healing
And
The cars stopped
The trains stopped
The busses stopped
The aircraft stopped

But the ego continued
And the self ran amok
Through the hallways of the mind…

Causing havoc
Ending all dreams of peace

What ensued?

The chaos of blame
The riotess of injustice
The murder of "I can't breathe"
And
The world stopped
And gasped
For air
For the life line
For hope…

Life understands
The shriek of fear
And the blame
That makes a game of life

Go on

Move on
Move away…

The love
Is
Almost over

The Resistant Heart

In the bitter rain
Assembled
By self
Without knowing
What or where or when...

Given over
To the little spark of love
Found unexpected
in the cracks
The wooly slippers
Or in the fresh bowl of soup

Do we ever unveil
Our real face?
Do we ever speak
With our true voice?
Do we ever sing
the song of our heart?

Somewhere
In between the life
and the longing
between the sun and the moon.
There must be an empty room filled
With the masks of lives

unlived...

Little One

She's buried deep in my soul.
She wants to get out.
She wants to be loved
And be held.
But I won't let her.
I've toughened her up.
I tell her she has to stay in there
I'm not going to let anyone see her.
They don't know she's there.

The little One.
Wants to speak but I won't let her.
Instead I pour vodka on her
And tell her to shut her face.
And the judges and the lawyers
And the bureaucrats never see her
They don't know that she's in there.

The little One
Wants to get out.
But I'm too tough for her.
I say "…close your eyes…
you don't want to see this!"
I can still hear her.
I haven't quite let her die.

And I cry because I miss her.
Do you?

Who am I?

I am alone
In a room
with no one else.

Outside.
Is fancy chaos
and loveless
Searching
Out there
The "successful" parade their wares
And even the sun has no place in the sky

The light falls along
On the grass and the trees
And no one seems to care
The successful man
Ties his tie
Buttons his coat
And hides his frightened eyes
Behind a mask of knowledge
That only he can see.
Never mind the madness
The grass still grows
day after day…
in silent praise
of the God
no one claims to know.

Fear

This writing is the only way it gets out.
I am no longer young, or stupid.
But the sun shines on all
Regardless.

Unwanted in the mud pile,
Confused in the classroom
Left vacant; like an empty coffee cup
Even the rocks outside my door Love
Better than me
It hurts to remember
Where I came from

Even the sand rejects me
Years in the courtroom
Locking up my screams.
In the middle of it all,
To look up there
At a judge, looking for justice
Screaming at the insanity …
Screaming at the play.
And the judge sits on his throne of equity
making decisions
As if it matters
No matter what, we are all dressed up to play our part
in this misery called magic…

Thought Police

They rise
In the quiet moments
when you least expect them
The holier than thou…
The purveyors of guilt
The know betters
The anti-thesis of freedom
The thought Police.

All will be monitored
says the wearer of white
the actress playing the part
As if unconscious thought should be removed
So all will think like her.

It must be right?
You, who sit in the treasured lap of wealth
and condemn all in your ignorance
to lecture and dismiss
the man on the street directing traffic
and the woman working at the 7-11.

All are dismissed
Because of appearance
She prods and accuses
challenges the space of all
from the luxury of unearned wealth
where there is room for riches and art
but no room for reason.

Nothing Matters

My log cabin
    Of the ground
      Sorrow rolls down…
Down to the pit
And despair comes next

I miss the ocean
But the cabin stands

In the end it doesn't matter.
They say, "there is so much magnificence"
But I can't see it
Through tears
I refuse to wipe away…
The light welcomes me
Blinking
Mocking me
The light belongs
To other people

The grass
In the light … green
Coming up
Only to get cut
Again and again.

The Incarceration of Belief

The voices say
In my existence is my guilt.
The voices seeking blame not solution,
Say I am at fault because of the colour of my skin
Focus on the past history
Not to learn but to erase it.
They in their ignorance
Seek someone to blame

Haphazardly assembled
Without knowing
What or when or where
Grasp on
To the tiny thread of fear
Found in the cracks
As each tear drops
Into the warm bowl of soup.
The mask is on

Do we ever unveil our true face?
Do we ever speak our real voice?
Do we ever sing from our heart?

Somewhere
In between the life and the longing
The sun and the moon.
There must be an empty room
Filled with the sadness of lives unlived.

Alive

The ego says, we are all alone here
The fear is close and heavy
I brush my teeth with it every night
And have it with my morning coffee.

Eyes open. Again.
What do I say?
"not another day"
"make it stop"
Every step is an effort.
Every meal turns my stomach.

I am too tired to close my eyes.
Sleep comes as long
As the itchy hands stay silent.

To the mirror - I seek refuge.
I stare at the lines in the face I don't know
The eyes of my Mother stare back at me
Asking a million questions;
Answering none.

Helpless

He doesn't drink.
I wonder why...
Sometimes drink
Is the only peace you get.

He is captive inside
And there he sits…
forgotten
Day upon day
Looking out the window
Onto the ocean
And people rushing past.

With a name
And a body
And an insane madness
That nobody knows

Somewhere deep inside
His soul is singing
But he cannot hear it
Through the sound of the ocean
And the silent screams
Of the only voice
He knows.

The Imprisoned Forgotten

He waited his whole life
For this
to recuse himself
From the insufferable race of life.

Former thoughts of freedom
Now are recognized
As truth sinks in
To the reality of hell.

Abandoned to nothing but the wall
And silence
The thought that life is over.
Silence, screaming to get out.

Who will hear him?

That life goes on without you.
to be forgotten
In the only place you think you can be.
Here.
Lost in unimportance.
Time is up.
Strength is gone.

Is it true?
The pretense.
The fear.
The loss.
The end.

Fear

In the hysteria of
Pandemic uncertainty
Youth fled, but
The sun shines on all
Regardless of youth or stupidity

Silent at the kitchen table
Confused in the classroom
Unwanted in the playground
Resting softly within
The totality of neglect

Even the rocks
Outside her door
Love better than she.
And the sand rejects her feet.
Spitting up drops of moisture
Unwelcome

Nothing lasts
Nothing is right....

Change of Mind

In silence
A prisoner of the past
Locked into regret
The epitome of loss

Don't speak of love
And turn away in anger
and slice my skin
with your bare, angry words

the ego, myself…lost
In a long-time struggle
With the hopelessness of right

The sign says "the end is near"
Don't forget
The pain ends when you say it does
You are its cause
The end may be today
Or tomorrow

Instead of running
From the demons
In your own mind

Love them.

The Fight

All is dead.
Everything is gone
Except those working
In fear;
In a love-hate relationship
With life.

Screaming at the inane
And the stupidity
And the play
And the actors…

When you know,
Deep inside
Where the pain comes from

No matter how much.
No matter how little.
We are all dressed up
To play our part
In this misery called 'MAGIC"

The Night

I wake in the night
To the silent voice
Of the God within
He and I; in reverence sit
And await the peace of morning.

The purveyors of fear
Cannot yet regulate the silence
Of mind and soul
Freedom lingers there.

In this night of prelude
Even the mouse is recognized
as he runs for cover

    Unmasked

Prayer is the antidote to insanity
    I ask for the answer
    I ask for a purpose
    Like being thirsty for water
    And never getting it
    …Knowing
    That you already are
    The answer
    To any question
    You have ever had.

The Cross

Fake
With a note about love
    Unmeant

Your perceived worthlessness
    Pains your soul
    And you spend your lifetime
    Trying to prove
    That this is so.

But, you must know
    That God loves you
    As much as anyone else

So, you open the letter
    And it appeals to your vanity
    Or it doesn't

And you put the cross of Jesus away
    Or you wear it

and forgiveness remains on a pedestal.
    Yet I cannot reach high enough
    I guess I'm not finished
Being your BITCH

    Just yet.

The Notebooks

Reflections, inspiration
    and the madness reflected
    within the scribblings
    of an ordinary mind.

I reflect on children peering into devices
    seeking love and salvation there.

    As my brother moves
Up closer to the God he created
    While condemning all else to hell
    For sin and guilt are real to him
    On the journey to Agape.

    Why should it matter
    To me?
    Whether he complicates love
    At least he talks love, not hate.

    The notebooks
    Are filled with nothing
    To the brim

    But I wouldn't part with them
    For all the money
    in the world.

The Circle Game

Round and round
The circle game;
I want to get off this ride
And move on.

Even now.
It takes all I am
To keep the vomit
From burning my throat.

Looking for life on Facebook
Seeking enlightenment in Hotmail
Playing the man with Tic-toc
The photographer on Instagram

The entertainment of the mind
Who knows when I will -
Miss the bend in the road
And finally reach home

Even then, who knows?
If it will be more of the same
Or worse?

CHANGE – Choose Love

Deep inside the heart,
intelligence of God
Rests the spirit of your divinity
Unquestioned.
Waiting.
Elevate your emotion
Clear your intention
Embrace it.

Freedom

Love is:
The misunderstood presence
Of your soul.
Love is:
Arriving back to oneness
After years of spent alone
Struggling
Apart from your essence.
To the heaven of true communion.
The freedom of honesty
The reality of truth.
Only together can love be understood.

No one can take you to heaven
It is a trip you make with God
At your side and within.
To understand love
Is to commune with your own spirit

He took me to freedom
From the bondage of hate
Hate for myself
Hate for life
Hate for others

Freedom
Is choosing to love
Instead.

Death of Illusion

Scared and hopeless
in a darkened room
The Lord of all stays by our side
And gently shows us love
As we are the light.

We play with guilt and suffering
like it's of great value
So, we give it much attention
and the figures flit back and forth
in a dream
you can't remember how you arrived
where you came from
or where you're going

You are quick to think of yourself as bad
the guilt and the sins pile up
And who can get it right?
Caution with threats of punishment
You, pretending your badness is real
Until you see that it is not.
Paying great attention to the look of the body
While the spirit goes unnoticed
The illusion remains…
the reality of your spirit is the only truth
It is carried around inside
You walk with God;
You walk in sacred space.

Acceptance

What do you see,
When you look in the mirror?
The faults?
The wrinkles?
The dirty hair?
Small eyes?
Blemishes and scars…

Accept your beauty.
Claim your brilliance
God loves you…
walk it out; with purpose
Love what God created.
Love you
The beautiful spirit
You.

There is more magnificence
In every cell of your body
Then there is in the whole universe.

It is you, who God loves
And the very least you can do
Is turn to God of all
And return the favour.

Perfection

We are one with God
his children
We are like our Father
Love creates
Like itself
Unchangeable
Look inside
For your creation itself
is the truth

beneath all fear
Your soul as part of the Father
sees with certainty
God's memory of us remains
And our function here is
To remember

let this memory return
The will of God be done
So we can be restored to sanity
And to be as God created us
Beyond doubt
Beyond harm
Whole
And

Free

Redemption

My Brother - stands beside me
Yet a stranger - My enemy
Unforgiven.
I do not know him - all I know is fear
Yet I attack him still
to keep my silent ego intact
But in my brother's hands
is the only way to peace

I see his madness
which I hate - because I share it.
and forgiveness that would heal it
gives way to fear
and I attack him yet again.

I need my brother's forgiveness.
For we will share together
either madness or heaven
the choice is ours.
And we will raise our eyes to God - for healing
together or not at all.

So, I give faith to my brother
for faith and hope and mercy are mine to give

I look on my brother as he is...
a gift from God. A gift of freedom

We stand together – or not at all
In heaven or hell -- the creation is ours.

The Christ Before Me

You sit alone
seeming helpless, without hope
attack flies from you
to those you can see
and back again
quick as day.
That is what you make
as the sun shines
with love on you,
constant and pure.

That is what you make
and you find a thousand reasons
to justify why this is so.

Oblivious to miracles all around
your heart, your love, your forgiveness.
The whole world that cannot be altered
to please your demands.
For righteousness.
The never-forgotten
miracle of the universal experience
hangs at the back of your mind.
Waiting for your eyes
to shine upon his truth.

You.

The you who stands in the hallway
unannounced.
The you that remains with me
through the centuries
and never fades.
Forever fixed.

Love entered into my heart
long before the creation of this body
which becomes the only soul I think I know.

The voice that speaks through me
Needs to speak through me
World without end...

the angel of the Lord appeared
not in the darkness of the night
but in the ever-present day
in the first light of morning
saying, "behold, I bring you tidings of great Joy
for today a Saviour is born,
Christ the Lord".

The Saviour is you.
The love is yours to give.
The birth is yours.
Every morning when you awake from sleep
you are born into the wonder of God's love.

The dream is over
wake
and see yourself
truly fixed
never forgotten.

Let it not stand in wait
or remain unforgiven.

In perfection
I see the Christ who stands before me
and humbled to witness him
as I witness to see myself
in the aura of the light of God.
That I would give to him

For true sight
sees as it gives
In perfect holiness.

Behold the Son of God
The Son of Man
Made perfect
in you.

The Unseen

In falseness
you try to capture moments
like drops of rain
when you miss the stillness
of the ever-present you
The you who is missed
That you try to hold
in a vain attempt
to hold the moment to you

You put your photographs on the wall
and look beyond the moment
fixated on a dream
you try to hold.

As the vanity of life
you forget who you are
Not the photograph
Not the face in the mirror

And you attack your brother
to make him guilty
So you can hold him to darkness
and create a hell for him
as you create your own
And you see the image of yourself as real.

Why do you attack God?
The very essence of yourself.
Wherefore the call for love remains
unanswered.

You make your brother, as yourself...
something to be feared

The enemy.
instead of the innocent
and you become
the enemy of reason.

Turn.
open your eyes
to see your brother
truly
see his love
see his innocence
see your saviour stand before you
as you are

what he does, you do
what he is you are

It is God's will
that his son be held and holy
saved and truly

As I open my eyes this day
and behold the light of my Father's creation

only for me
only for you
only for us

in gratitude for all that is

I say:

**"My Father's will be done
on earth as it is in heaven
love
Forgive
Behold the Son of God"**

Pyramid

In a dream
Past midnight
I stood in white
atop a glass pyramid
and asked
The Creator

I asked him
"why the suffering?"
'why the pain?"
"why the death?'

He looked at me
with crystal blue eyes

and said:
"don't you think,
it's time you started
to trust me?"
There is
Only love.

All there is

This brilliant moment
Of you
Is the be all and the end all
Not to be suffered through
Not to be dismissed
Understand
Life is your gift

This is your creation
The empty slate of you
The birth, growth
Death and resurrection
Is in the composite now.

Walk down
To the river of your soul
Bathe in it
The wonder
The divinity
Let go of the shore
Let the river take you

Have faith in this moment
Reach for the light
This moment is your redeemer
Beside you
Making all things right
The perfection cancels despair
Removes all fear
From you and all of life
By your creation
Your choice.

Your life is now.
In this moment
Accept it
Love it
It is
All there is of time.

Kindness

People are not kind
To each other.
yet
Kindness is our very nature.

Feel
peacefulness
Relax
You are the sacred
Under it all
People are good

Somewhere
Someone
Would give you the shirt
Off their back
…

Turn from it

You create perfection
In things
Yet inside
Your soul is screaming

The world outside
Of chaos and struggle
Remembers not
The being
In the heart of God

In his heart

The love
Being held
In the hand of my Father

This is your right
This is your freedom
This is your dignity

It's who you are
Love is present
And you can never be separate
From the love and presence
Of God.

The Christ in Me

All of humanity
Has the connection
To love
Through choice,
Through thought
And eventual action

The Spirit of Christ

Inside
Is the hope of this world.
The Christ inside
Is strong

The physical power
And presence of our god

The creation of life
Of me

Salvation

We are free
We are not the scourge
We are not the cancer on the planet
There is something wonderful
In our being
Here

How about: we are good
How about: we are success
How about: we are beautiful
We are perfect.
Courageous
Survivors
Unharmable

How about:
We are responsible
For what we are
We create our life
The universe is a friendly place

And I am its creator.

Of My Life

Soul of my life
Energy of the spirit
Home in me
Where is my perfection?

Blame is added
To the source of creation
Without beginning
Without end
Creator of all

Our suffering is heard
War, riot, poverty, guilt, separation
Disease
The lord reaches
For us
To heal and to bless
All creatures
Days run to weeks,
months and years
It has been so long
Since I've seen myself
I don't even know if I am still here.

The Word After

The belief in the reality
And permanence - Of our physical body
Pleasure seeking and avoiding of pain
In its pursuit, it decorates and adorns
This body and works to obtain success
And things that will ultimately turn to dust
Like this body itself
So, you make the dream seem real
And react to the effect you have created
While the cause of the dream
You - Remain unencumbered with responsibility
Perceive the dream as separate from yourself
And done to you.
Into eternity where all is one
There occurred an idea of insanity
That part of God can attack itself
Or make its brother an enemy
Do not assign him your guilt…to keep your innocence
The secret to your peace is clear
You are creating your life
Take responsibility for its errors
And in the simple truth made clear:
Forgive the world your guilt
Set yourself free
We stand together or not at all
The choice is ours.

Meditation

Sit quietly or lie down
Close your eyes
Listen to the sounds off in the distance:
The whirring of the fan, a car going by
The sound of rain gently falling outside.
Focus your attention on that sound

Listen

Bring your attention to the sounds closer to you
The sound of the light buzzing in the room you're in
People talking, music playing
--
Follow the sound inward
Bring your attention to the air going in and out of your lungs
As you breathe naturally

Focus on the beats of your heart

Listen

Visualize the space inside the palms of your hands

Pay attention to the movement of energy inside you

Sit - Observe
Wait
In the stillness

REMEMBER

WHO

YOU

ARE

Manufactured by Amazon.ca
Bolton, ON